AFTER·SCHOOL SNACK COOKBOOK

Meredith® Corporation
Des Moines, Iowa

AFTER-SCHOOL SNACK COOKBOOK

MEREDITH CORPORATION PRINT ADVANTAGE
Vice President, Production: Bruce Heston
National Sales Director: Linda Hyden
Associate Director, Production: Doug Johnston

WATERBURY PUBLICATIONS, INC.
Editorial Director: Lisa Kingsley
Associate Editor: Tricia Laning
Creative Director: Ken Carlson
Associate Design Director: Doug Samuelson
Senior Designer: Chad Jewell
Production Coordinator: Mindy Samuelson
Contributing Editor: Mary Williams
Contributing Copy Editor: Gretchen Kauffman
Contributing Proofreaders: Terri Fredrickson, Peg Smith
Contributing Indexer: Elizabeth T. Parson

MEREDITH PUBLISHING GROUP
President: Jack Griffin
Executive Vice President: Andy Sareyan
Vice President, Manufacturing: Bruce Heston

MEREDITH CORPORATION
Chairman of the Board: William T. Kerr
President and Chief Executive Officer: Stephen M. Lacy

In Memoriam: E.T. Meredith III (1933–2003)

All of us at Meredith Print Advantage are dedicated to providing you with information and ideas to enhance your home. We welcome your comments and suggestions. Write to us at: Meredith Print Advantage, 1716 Locust St., Des Moines, IA 50309-3023.

Table of Contents

4

Who's Hungry?

If your stomach is growling even though you scarfed down everything on your lunch plate, then get a load of the *After-School Snack Cookbook*! Just for kids, it's a cookbook that's filled with awesome snacks to fight off hunger and refuel your body with energy to keep you going.

You won't find any boring grown-up snacks here. The *After-School Snack Cookbook* is jam-packed with totally cool recipes. Can't wait to eat? Guzzle down a Rocky Road Malt that's ready in 10 minutes. Throw a crazy TGIF party with a plateful of Nacho Melters. And if you really need to attack your hunger, try All-Star Pizza to turn your snack into a meal.

So if you're tired of listening to your stomach growl, start cooking. Just grab the ingredients and follow the directions. You'll be amazed by what great-tasting stuff you can make.

Ready Now Snacks

When you arrive home from school and you're starving, these 10-minute snacks will stop those hunger pangs instantly.

Crunchy Fruit Sundaes

If cereal and fruit top your favorite snack list, you'll love this good-for-you combo of fresh berries, grapes, and cereal. Yogurt makes it creamy.

Ingredients

1   cup assorted fresh fruit such as blueberries, grapes, strawberries, and/or bananas

1   6-ounce carton vanilla low-fat yogurt

½   to 1 cup ready-to-eat cereal, such as round toasted oat cereal

1   tablespoon almonds or walnuts, if you like

Utensils

cutting board

sharp knife

small bowl

measuring spoons

small spoon

measuring cups

2 cereal bowls

How to Make It

1   If you are using the strawberries, place them on the cutting board. Use the knife to cut off the green tops. Throw the green tops away. Cut the strawberries into bite-size pieces. If you are using the bananas, remove the peels and throw away. Place the bananas on the cutting board. Use the knife to cut into bite-size pieces.

2   Divide the yogurt in half and spoon each half into a serving bowl. Divide cereal and fruit in half and place into bowls with yogurt. If you like, top with almonds or walnuts. Serve sundaes immediately. Makes 2 servings.

Winning Apple Crisp

Keep your growling stomach quiet with this warm snack and become a kitchen champion. If you want to go a little nuts, add the almonds.

Ingredients

- 1 4-ounce snack-size container unsweetened applesauce
- ⅛ teaspoon apple pie spice or ground cinnamon
- 2 tablespoons sugar-coated cornflakes or round toasted multigrain cereal
- 1 tablespoon sliced almonds, pecan pieces, or walnut pieces, if you like

Utensils

small spoons

6-ounce microwave-safe custard cup or small bowl

measuring spoons

hot pads

How to Make It

1 Uncover applesauce container. Spoon applesauce into the microwave-safe custard cup or bowl. Use the small spoon to stir in apple pie spice or cinnamon.

2 Place custard cup with applesauce in the microwave. Microwave, uncovered, on 100% power (high) for 15 to 30 seconds or until warm. Use hot pads to remove custard cup from microwave; stir applesauce. Sprinkle the cereal over the warm applesauce. If you like, sprinkle with nuts. Eat while warm. Makes 1 serving.

Strawberry-Apple Crisp: Make as directed above, except do not add the apple pie spice or cinnamon to the applesauce. Instead stir 1 teaspoon strawberry preserves into the cold applesauce. Heat and serve as directed above in Step 2.

Dip and Eat

Finger foods rule in this fun-to-eat snack. Sausage, cheese, bread, and veggies turn into delicious dunkers when served with tomato sauce.

Ingredients

- 1 ounce smoked turkey sausage
- 1 ounce mozzarella or provolone cheese
- 1 ounce Italian bread
- ½ of a small zucchini, 1 carrot, ½ cup broccoli florets, ½ of a medium green sweet pepper, and/or ½ cup grape or cherry tomatoes
- ¼ cup tomato sauce
- ⅛ teaspoon dried Italian seasoning
- Dash garlic powder

Utensils

- cutting board
- sharp knife
- serving plate
- measuring cups
- measuring spoons
- small bowl
- small spoon

How to Make It

1. On the cutting board, use the sharp knife to cut sausage into bite-size slices. On the same cutting board, use the sharp knife to cut the cheese into bite-size cubes. On the cutting board, use the sharp knife to cut the bread into bite-size pieces. On the cutting board, use the sharp knife to cut the zucchini, carrot, and/or sweet pepper into bite-size pieces. Arrange sausage, cheese, bread, and all the vegetables on the plate.

2. Put the tomato sauce, Italian seasoning, and garlic powder in the small bowl. Stir with a small spoon until combined.

3. To eat, dip the sausage, cheese, bread, and vegetable pieces in the tomato mixture. Makes 1 serving.

13

Crunchy PB & A Wraps

Get ready to wrap and roll! When you're in a hurry, fix these tortillas filled with peanut butter and apple in minutes, then take them with you.

Ingredients

- 2   7- to 8-inch flour tortillas
- ¼   cup peanut butter
- ½   cup chopped apple
- 2   tablespoons low-fat granola

Utensils

cutting board

measuring cups

table knife

measuring spoons

sharp knife

How to Make It

1 Place the tortillas on a cutting board. Use the table knife to spread peanut butter over each tortilla. Sprinkle each with half of the apple and half of the granola.

2 Roll up the tortillas tightly. Place the tortilla rolls with the seam sides down on the cutting board. Use the sharp knife to cut the tortilla rolls in half. Makes 2 wraps.

Fruit Waffle Cones

Bring some friends home from school and wow them with a neat treat.
Pile pudding and fresh fruit into sweet, crispy waffle cones.

Ingredients

1   4-serving-size package
    instant lemon,
    vanilla, or white
    chocolate pudding
    mix

1⅓   cups milk

1   cup fresh fruit, such
    as blueberries,
    sliced kiwifruit,
    sliced strawberries,
    raspberries, and/or
    sliced bananas

4   waffle ice cream cones
    or large waffle ice
    cream bowls

Utensils

measuring cups

medium bowl

wire whisk or rotary beater

large spoon

How to Make It

1 Put the pudding mix and the milk into the bowl. Use the wire whisk or rotary beater to whisk or beat mixture about 2 minutes or until it starts to thicken.

2 Spoon the fruit into cones. Top with the pudding. Serve immediately. Makes 4 cones.

Blaze-a-Trail Mix

Before hitting the trail, shake together this tasty snack mix. You'll have enough for a week's worth of after-school adventures.

Ingredients

- 2 cups honey graham cereal
- 1 cup tiny marshmallows
- 1 cup peanuts
- ½ cup semisweet chocolate pieces
- ½ cup raisins

Utensils

measuring cups

large storage container with lid

How to Make It

1 Put the cereal, marshmallows, peanuts, chocolate pieces, and raisins in the storage container. Cover and shake to mix. Store in a cool, dry place for up to 2 weeks. Makes 5 cups.

Choco·Nutty Spread

Sandwich this yummy chocolate and peanut butter spread between cookies or crackers. Or stir in a little more yogurt and use it as a dip for the fruit.

Ingredients

½ cup chunky peanut butter

¼ cup plain low-fat yogurt

¼ cup chocolate-flavored syrup

½ teaspoon vanilla

32 vanilla wafers or 16 graham cracker squares

1 cup assorted fresh fruit, such as pineapple chunks, sliced strawberries, sliced bananas, and/or sliced apples, if you like

Utensils

measuring cups

measuring spoons

medium bowl

wooden spoon

table knife

container with a lid, if you like

How to Make It

1 Put the peanut butter, yogurt, chocolate syrup, and vanilla in the bowl. Use the wooden spoon to stir the mixture until it is smooth and well mixed.

2 Use the table knife to spread the chocolate spread on the flat sides of half of the vanilla wafers or graham cracker squares. Top with the remaining wafers with flat sides down or graham cracker squares. If you like, serve with fresh fruit. Store leftover spread in a tightly covered container in the refrigerator up to 3 days. Makes 1 cup spread (16 cookie sandwiches).

Rocky Road Malts

You won't find any rocks in these frosty shakes—just great chocolate and peanut butter taste. Float marshmallow crème, peanuts, and cookies on top.

Ingredients

- 1 quart chocolate ice cream
- ⅓ to ½ cup milk
- ⅓ cup chocolate instant malted milk powder
- ¼ cup creamy peanut butter
- Marshmallow crème, if you like
- Coarsely chopped peanuts, if you like
- Miniature sandwich cookies, if you like

Utensils

- ice cream scoop
- electric blender
- measuring cups
- rubber scraper
- 4 glasses

How to Make It

1 Use the ice cream scoop to put half of the ice cream in the blender. Add milk, malted milk powder, and peanut butter. Cover the blender with the lid. Blend on high speed until smooth. Stop the blender. Scoop the remaining ice cream into the blender. Cover the blender and blend until smooth. If necessary, stop the blender and scrape down the sides with the rubber scraper. If necessary, add additional milk until mixture is the desired consistency.

2 To serve, spoon into 4 glasses. If you like, top with marshmallow crème, chopped peanuts, and miniature sandwich cookies. Makes 4 malts.

Easy as ABC Cookies

Fight off after-school munchies by devouring an alphabet you can eat. If you don't have letter-shape cookies, any shortbread or sugar cookie will do.

Ingredients

- 2 ounces cream cheese (tub-style)
- 1 tablespoon strawberry preserves
- Red food coloring, if you like
- 32 plain alphabet cookies and/or chocolate shortbread cookies

Utensils

- measuring spoons
- small bowl
- wooden spoon
- table knife

How to Make It

1 Put the cream cheese and preserves in the small bowl. Stir with the wooden spoon until the mixture is smooth. If you like, stir in a drop of red food coloring.

2 Use the table knife to spread cream cheese mixture on the flat sides of half of the cookies. Top with the remaining cookies with the flat sides down.

Tropical Salad

Pretend you're exploring a tropical island when you spoon into these sweet, juicy fruit cups.

Ingredients

- 1 8-ounce can pineapple chunks (juice pack), chilled
- ½ cup miniature marshmallows
- ½ cup sour cream
- 1 11-ounce can mandarin orange sections, chilled
- 1 tablespoon toasted shredded coconut, if you like

Utensils

- colander
- can opener
- measuring cups
- medium bowl
- wooden spoon
- rubber scraper
- measuring spoons, if you like

How to Make It

1 Put the colander in the sink. Put the pineapple and liquid in the colander and let the liquid drain into the sink. Put the pineapple, marshmallows, and sour cream in the bowl. Use the wooden spoon to combine.

2 Put the mandarin oranges and liquid in the colander and let the liquid drain into the sink. Use the rubber scraper to gently stir the mandarin oranges into the pineapple mixture. If you like, sprinkle with coconut. Makes 4 servings.

Double·Dippin' Fruit

Double-dipping is allowed with this fun-to-eat snack. Dip the fruit twice—once in caramel sauce and then in the crunchy granola.

Ingredients

1 4-ounce container vanilla pudding (prepared pudding cup)

3 tablespoons caramel ice cream topping

½ teaspoon vanilla

¼ of an 8-ounce container frozen light whipped dessert topping, thawed

¾ cup granola

Assorted fresh fruit such as sliced apples, banana chunks, and/or strawberries

Utensils

measuring spoons

medium bowl

small spoon

rubber scraper

2 serving bowls

measuring cups

How to Make It

1 To make the caramel dip, uncover pudding container. Put pudding, caramel topping, and vanilla in the medium bowl; stir until smooth with the spoon. Use the rubber scraper to gently stir in the whipped topping.

2 To serve, pour the caramel dip into a serving bowl. Use the rubber scraper to scrape all of the dip into the bowl. Put granola in another serving bowl. Serve caramel dip and granola with fruit. Dip fruit in caramel dip, then in granola. Makes 6 servings.

Kickin' S'mores

The filling in these gooey treats might squeeze out a little, but with the combo of chocolate and marshmallow, the drips are delicious!

Ingredients

- 4 graham crackers, quartered
- 4 teaspoons fudge ice cream topping
- 64 miniature marshmallows (about ¾ cup)
- 4 teaspoons strawberry jam

Utensils

- microwave-safe plate
- table knife
- measuring spoons
- measuring cups
- small spoon

How to Make It

1 Place 8 of the graham cracker quarters on the microwave-safe plate. Use the knife to spread the ice cream topping evenly on the crackers. Place 8 marshmallows on each cracker.

2 Microwave, uncovered, on 100% power (high) for 30 seconds. Spoon the jam evenly over the marshmallows and quickly top with the remaining graham cracker quarters. Serve the s'mores immediately. Makes 4 servings.

Peanut Butter S'mores: Prepare s'mores as directed above, except use chocolate graham cracker squares and substitute peanut butter for ice cream topping. Don't use the jam.

Pretzel Lollipops

You'll be able to lick any snack attack with these sweet and salty pretzels. Peanut butter glues the cereal to the rods.

Ingredients

¾ cup chocolate-flavored puffed corn cereal and/or sweetened fruit-flavored round toasted cereal

2 tablespoons creamy peanut butter

4 pretzel rods

Utensils

waxed paper

measuring cups

measuring spoons

thin metal spatula

storage container with lid

How to Make It

1 Lay the waxed paper on the counter. Spread the cereal on waxed paper. Set aside.

2 Use the metal spatula to spread peanut butter in a thin layer over half of each pretzel rod. Roll each rod in the cereal so it sticks to the peanut butter. Eat right away or put rods in an airtight container and store at room temperature for up to 1 day. Makes 4 snacks.

Fruit Smoothies

Skate through hunger by slurping down one of these far-out fruit smoothies that are good for you.

Ingredients

- 2 small ripe bananas
- 2 6-ounce cartons vanilla low-fat yogurt
- 1 cup sliced fresh strawberries or unsweetened frozen strawberries
- 1 cup fresh mixed berries, such as raspberries, blueberries, and/or blackberries, or unsweetened frozen mixed berries

Utensils

cutting board

table knife

measuring cups

blender or food processor

rubber scraper

4 tall glasses

How to Make It

1 Peel the bananas; throw away the peels. Put the bananas on the cutting board. Use the table knife to cut the bananas into chunks.

2 Put the bananas, yogurt, strawberries, and the mixed berries in a blender or food processor. Cover the blender or food processor with the lid. Blend or process on high speed until the mixture is smooth. If necessary, stop the machine and use the rubber scraper to scrape down sides. Pour into tall glasses. Makes 4 smoothies.

Meals as Snacks

If you're running on empty after school, fill up with one of these mealtime favorites. You'll still have room for dinner later.

Three-Ring Pizzas

Just as a three-ring circus thrills you with fantastic feats, these circular treats wow your taste buds with fun in every bite.

Ingredients

Shortening

1 1-pound loaf frozen bread dough, thawed

All-purpose flour

1 8-ounce can pizza sauce

1½ cups shredded pizza cheese (6 ounces)

½ of a 3.5-ounce package sliced pepperoni

6 slices pizza-style Canadian bacon (1½ inches in diameter)

1 medium green sweet pepper, seeded and cut into 6 rings

2 yellow or red cherry tomatoes

Utensils

2 large baking sheets

large cutting board

sharp knife

rolling pin

ruler

fork

spoon

hot pads

2 wire cooling racks

How to Make It

1 Turn on the oven to 425°F. Grease the baking sheets with the shortening. Place the bread dough on the cutting board. Use the sharp knife to cut the dough into 6 even pieces. Shape each piece into a ball. Sprinkle the cutting board with flour. On the floured surface, flatten each ball; use the rolling pin to roll each ball into a 6-inch circle. Arrange 3 dough circles on each baking sheet. Use the fork to poke holes in the dough.

2 Use the spoon to put pizza sauce on the dough circles. Spread the sauce evenly over the circles. Top with cheese. Arrange pepperoni slices in a ring around the outside edge of each pizza. Place a Canadian bacon slice in center of each pizza. Top each pizza with a sweet pepper ring.

3 Slice each cherry tomato into thirds; place one piece in the center of each Canadian bacon slice.

4 Put pizzas in the oven. Bake about 10 minutes or until edges are lightly browned. Turn off the oven. Use hot pads to remove baking sheets from oven. Let stand on wire racks for 5 minutes. Makes 6 pizzas.

All·Star Pizza

Let this pizza for two be your number-one pick for a delicious snacktime lineup that will win big every time you make it.

Ingredients

1 4-ounce Italian bread shell (such as Boboli brand)

2 tablespoons pizza sauce

2 slices Canadian bacon or large pepperoni (1 to 2 ounces)

3 thin slices mozzarella cheese and/or cheddar cheese (1½ ounces)

Utensils

pizza pan or baking sheet

measuring spoons

spoon

cutting board

sharp knife or kitchen scissors

ruler

hot pads

wire cooling rack

pancake turner

2 serving plates

How to Make It

1 Turn on the oven to 425°F. Put the Italian bread shell on the pizza pan or baking sheet.

2 Drizzle the pizza sauce on the bread shell. Use the back of the spoon to spread the pizza sauce over the bread shell to within ½ inch of the edge.

3 Put the Canadian bacon or pepperoni slices on the cutting board. Use the sharp knife or scissors to cut the meat into ¾-inch-wide strips. Arrange the meat strips on the pizza.

4 Place the cheese on the center of the pizza, leaving a large circle of sauce around the edge of the pizza.

5 Put the pan in the oven. Bake for 5 to 7 minutes or until pizza is hot. Turn off the oven. Use the hot pads to remove the pizza pan from the oven. Place the pan on the wire rack.

6 Cut the pizza into wedges with the sharp knife. Use the pancake turner to put the pizza slices on serving plates. Serve immediately. Makes 2 servings.

Perfect Ten Tostadas

Earn a perfect score when you serve this tostada piled high with chicken, veggies, and cheese. It's a snack to flip for!

Ingredients

- 1½ cups (½ of an 18-ounce tub) taco sauce with shredded chicken
- 4 6-inch tostada shells
- ¾ cup shredded carrot, packaged shredded broccoli (broccoli slaw mix), and/or canned black beans, rinsed and drained
- ⅓ cup shredded Colby and Monterey Jack cheese

Utensils

measuring cups

small saucepan

wooden spoon

hot pads

serving platter

How to Make It

1 Put the chicken mixture in the saucepan. Place the pan on the burner. Turn the burner to medium heat. Cook until the chicken is heated through, stirring now and then with the wooden spoon. Turn off the burner. Use the hot pads to remove the pan from the burner.

2 Place the tostada shells on the serving platter. Use the wooden spoon to divide the heated chicken mixture evenly among the tostada shells. Sprinkle each tostada with carrot, broccoli, and/or beans. Sprinkle each tostada with cheese. Makes 4 tostadas.

Rockin' Tunawiches

Make a tuna sandwich rock by cutting the bread into fish shapes. Use any shape cutters you like to switch your theme.

Ingredients

- 1   3-ounce can chunk white tuna (water pack)
- ½   cup packaged shredded cabbage with carrot (coleslaw mix)
- 2   tablespoons plain low-fat yogurt
- 2   tablespoons bottled ranch salad dressing
- 8   thin slices whole grain bread
-     Raisins, if you like

Utensils

colander

can opener

small bowl

fork

measuring cups

spoon

measuring spoons

cutting board

4- to 4½-inch fish-shape or other shape cookie cutter

table knife

How to Make It

1 Put the colander in the sink. Open the can of tuna. Put the tuna in the colander and let the liquid drain into the sink. Put the tuna in the small bowl. Use the fork to break up the tuna. Add cabbage mix. Stir with the spoon to combine. Stir in yogurt and salad dressing.

2 Place bread slices on the cutting board. Using the cookie cutter, cut fish or other shapes from bread slices. Save bread scraps for another use. Use the table knife to spread tuna mixture on half of the bread shapes. Top with remaining bread shapes. If you like, decorate sandwiches with raisins for eyes. Makes 4 sandwiches.

Mini Submarines

Feeling drained after school? These miniature submarine sandwiches will revive your energy quicker than a plunge in the sea.

Ingredients

3   6-inch unsliced French-style rolls

Yellow mustard

1   tomato

6   ounces thinly sliced cooked ham, roast beef, or turkey

3   slices provolone, mozzarella, or Swiss cheese (3 ounces), halved

6   small lettuce leaves

Utensils

cutting board

sharp knife

table knife

How to Make It

1 On the cutting board, use the sharp knife to carefully make a slit about 4 inches long on the top of each roll. With your fingers, hollow out a ¾-inch-wide strip of bread along the slit. Use the table knife to spread the inside of each roll with mustard. Set the rolls aside. On the same cutting board, use the sharp knife to cut the tomato into thin wedges.

2 Divide the ham and cheese evenly among the rolls. Add a lettuce leaf and some of the tomato wedges to each roll. Cut the rolls in half. Makes 6 sandwiches.

Ham Quesadillas

Say adios to your hunger pangs. Stuff this Mexican-style snack with a filling of ham and your favorite cheese. Choose Swiss, Monterey Jack, or cheddar.

Ingredients

- 2   7- to 8-inch whole wheat, spinach, tomato, or plain flour tortillas
- 1/3   cup shredded Swiss, Monterey Jack, or cheddar cheese
- 2   ounces thinly sliced cooked ham
- 1/3   cup chopped tomato
- 1   tablespoon sliced green onion tops, if you like

Utensils

cutting board

measuring cups

measuring spoons, if you use green onion tops

10-inch nonstick skillet

pancake turner

hot pads

2 serving plates

sharp knife

How to Make It

1 Put the tortillas on the cutting board. Sprinkle cheese over half of each tortilla. Top with ham, tomato, and, if you like, green onion tops. Fold tortillas in half. Press tortillas gently.

2 Put quesadillas in the skillet. Place the skillet on the burner. Turn the burner to medium heat. Cook for 1½ to 2 minutes or until tortillas are lightly browned. Turn the quesadillas over with the pancake turner. Cook until bottoms are lightly browned. Turn off burner. Use hot pads to remove the skillet from the burner. Remove the quesadillas from the skillet and put on serving plates. Cut into wedges with the sharp knife. Makes 2 servings.

Crazy Bean Burritos

If your stomach is feeling empty, refuel it with a loaded burrito and you'll be saying "Cool beans!"

Ingredients

4   10-inch flour tortillas

1   16-ounce can refried beans or one 15-ounce can black beans

¼   teaspoon ground cumin

½   cup salsa or picante sauce

½   cup shredded taco cheese or cheddar cheese (2 ounces)

½   cup lettuce torn in small pieces

Additional salsa or picante sauce, if you like

Utensils

foil

can opener

colander, if you use black beans

potato masher, if you use black beans

medium bowl, if you use black beans

medium saucepan

measuring spoons

wooden spoon

hot pads

measuring cups

How to Make It

1 Turn on the oven to 350°F. Wrap tortillas in foil. Put wrapped tortillas in oven. Bake about 10 minutes or until tortillas are warm.

2 While the tortillas warm, open the can of beans. (If you are using black beans, pour beans into a colander, rinse with cold water, and drain well. Put black beans into the bowl and mash them with the potato masher.) Put refried beans or mashed black beans into the saucepan. Stir cumin into beans with the wooden spoon. Put the saucepan on the burner. Turn the burner to medium heat. Cook about 5 minutes or until beans are warm, stirring now and then with the wooden spoon. Turn off burner. Use hot pads to remove saucepan from burner.

3 Turn off the oven. Use hot pads to remove the tortillas from the oven.

4 Spoon about ¼ cup of the beans near one edge of each tortilla. Add 2 tablespoons salsa or picante sauce, 2 tablespoons cheese, and 2 tablespoons lettuce. Roll tortillas around filling. If you like, serve with additional salsa or picante sauce. Makes 4 burritos.

PB & Berry Pockets

This protein-packed pouch will keep you running in tip-top shape through all of your afternoon activities.

Ingredients

- 2 large whole wheat or white pita bread rounds, halved crosswise
- ½ cup chunky peanut butter
- ¼ cup raisins
- 1 cup sliced or chopped fresh strawberries
- 2 tablespoons dry roasted sunflower kernels

Utensils

measuring cups

table knife

small spoon

measuring spoon

How to Make It

1 Use your fingers to carefully split each pita half open (but do not break into 2 pieces) to form a pocket.

2 Use the knife to spread peanut butter inside pita pockets. Use the spoon to divide raisins, strawberries, and sunflower kernels among pockets. Makes 4 pockets.

Totally Tacos

Transform a snack into a fiesta with these tasty, full-of-meat tacos. Pick and choose your favorite toppings—sour cream, tomato, salsa, or extra cheese.

Ingredients

12   ounces lean ground beef

½   cup salsa

½   teaspoon dried oregano, crushed

4   lettuce leaves

8   regular-size taco shells*

¾   cup shredded cheddar cheese (3 ounces)

Sour cream, chopped tomato, and extra salsa, if you like

Utensils

large skillet with lid

wooden spoon

hot pads

colander

medium bowls

measuring cups

measuring spoons

spoon

tongs

hot pads

How to Make It

1 Put ground beef in the skillet; use the wooden spoon to break up meat. Put the skillet on a burner. Turn the burner to medium-high heat. Cook until no pink color is left in meat, stirring now and then with the wooden spoon. This will take 8 to 10 minutes. Turn off burner. Use hot pads to remove skillet from burner.

2 Place colander over bowl. Spoon meat into the colander and let the fat drain into the bowl. Spoon meat back into skillet. Put fat in a container to throw away.

3 Stir the ½ cup salsa and the oregano into meat. Cover skillet; put skillet on a burner. Turn burner to medium heat. Cook for 5 minutes, stirring with wooden spoon after 3 minutes. Turn off burner. Use hot pads to remove skillet from burner. Put meat mixture in a clean bowl.

4 While meat mixture is cooking, tear or cut lettuce into bite-size pieces.

5 To make tacos, spoon meat mixture into taco shells. Add lettuce and cheese. If you like, top tacos with sour cream, chopped tomato, and extra salsa. Makes 4 servings.

*Tip: If you like, make taco shells crisp by placing them on a baking sheet and warming them in a 350°F oven for 5 to 7 minutes or until crisp. Turn off oven. Use hot pads to remove baking sheet from oven. Use tongs to put shells on a cool plate.

Hot Ham Sandwiches

Power up grilled cheese sandwiches by adding ham and dipping them in a mixture of egg and milk before cooking them in a skillet.

Ingredients

4   slices firm wheat bread, white bread, or sourdough bread

2   to 3 teaspoons Dijon-style mustard

2   ounces thinly sliced cooked ham

2   slices Swiss cheese (2 ounces)

1   egg

¼   cup milk

Nonstick cooking spray

Utensils

table knife

shallow bowl

fork

nonstick griddle or large skillet

pancake turner

hot pads

2 serving plates

How to Make It

1 Use the knife to spread mustard on 2 of the bread slices. Top with ham and cheese. Place remaining bread slices on top of ham and cheese. Crack the egg into the bowl. Add milk. Beat with fork until ingredients are well mixed.

2 Coat the griddle or skillet with nonstick cooking spray. Put the skillet on the burner. Turn the burner to medium heat. Dip each sandwich in milk mixture; turn the sandwich over and dip the second side. Place sandwiches on the griddle or in the skillet. Cook until bottoms are golden. This will take 1 to 2 minutes. Use the pancake turner to turn sandwiches over and cook until the second sides are golden and the cheese melts. Turn off burner. Use hot pads to remove skillet from heat. Use the pancake turner to remove sandwiches from skillet and place on plates. Cut in halves with the table knife. Makes 2 sandwiches.

Double·Decker Stacks

These tortillas are stacked to the max with cream cheese and your choice of apples, pears, or bananas.

Ingredients

- ½ of an 8-ounce tub plain or strawberry cream cheese, softened
- ½ teaspoon finely shredded orange peel
- 2 to 3 teaspoons milk
- 1 medium apple, pear, and/or banana
- 3 8-inch plain flour or whole wheat tortillas
- ¼ cup chopped toasted almonds, pecans, or walnuts, if you like

Utensils

box grater

measuring spoons

small bowl

spoon

sharp knife

cutting board

table knife

plate

How to Make It

1 Put cream cheese, orange peel, and milk in the small bowl. Stir with the spoon until mixed. Save until Step 3.

2 If using apple or pear, on the cutting board, use the sharp knife to cut out the core and thinly slice the apple or pear. If using banana, peel and use cutting board and sharp knife to slice.

3 Put the tortillas on a clean work surface. Spread cream cheese mixture onto tortillas using the table knife. Place one tortilla, cream cheese side up, on the plate. Top with half of the fruit slices. If you like, sprinkle with half the nuts. Add another layer of tortilla, the remaining fruit slices, and, if you like, the remaining nuts. Top with remaining tortilla with the cream cheese side down. To serve, cut into wedges with the sharp knife. Makes 4 servings.

TGIF Snacks

It's Friday and time to party! Making and eating these festive snacks with friends is the perfect way to kick off the weekend.

Kicker Cheese Ball

Score a perfect goal with this cheesy creation. Team it with crackers and wedges of fresh fruit.

Ingredients

1   3-ounce package
    cream cheese
1¼ cups shredded taco
    cheese
    Dash bottled hot
    pepper sauce
    Assorted crackers
    Apple or pear wedges

Utensils

medium mixing bowl

measuring cups

electric mixer

rubber scraper

plastic wrap

serving plate

How to Make It

1   Put cream cheese and 1 cup of the taco cheese in a
    medium mixing bowl. Let stand at room temperature for
30 minutes.

2   Add bottled hot pepper sauce to the cheese mixture
    in the mixing bowl. Beat with the electric mixer
on medium speed until combined, stopping the mixer
occasionally and scraping the bowl with the rubber scraper.
Stop the mixer.

3   Cover the bowl with plastic wrap. Place the bowl in the
    refrigerator for 4 to 24 hours.

4   Use your hands to shape the cheese mixture into a
    3-inch ball. Roll the ball in the remaining
¼ cup cheese to coat. Place the ball on the serving plate.
Let stand about 15 minutes before serving.

5   Serve cheese ball with crackers and apple or pear
    wedges. Makes ⅔ cup (five 2-tablespoon servings).

Slam Dunk Veggies

Better make lots of these crispy-coated vegetables. You'll love dipping them in pizza sauce and munching them.

Ingredients

Nonstick cooking spray

⅔ cup seasoned fine dry bread crumbs

2 tablespoons grated Parmesan cheese

⅛ teaspoon salt

2 egg whites

1 tablespoon milk

4 cups cauliflower florets and/or broccoli florets

2 tablespoons butter or margarine, melted

1 15-ounce can pizza sauce

Utensils

15×10×1-inch baking pan

2 large plastic bags

measuring cups

measuring spoons

small microwave-safe bowl

hot pads

wooden spoon

How to Make It

1 Turn on oven to 400°F. Lightly coat the baking pan with cooking spray. Save until Step 2. In a large plastic bag combine bread crumbs, cheese, and salt. In another large plastic bag combine egg whites and milk.

2 Add vegetables to the plastic bag with the egg mixture. Close bag and shake to coat well. Add vegetables to plastic bag with the crumb mixture. Close bag and shake to coat the vegetables with crumbs. Place coated vegetables in the baking pan. Drizzle melted butter over vegetables.

3 Put baking pan in oven. Bake for 20 minutes or until golden brown, stirring twice with the wooden spoon; use hot pads when removing the pan from the oven each time. Turn off the oven. Meanwhile, put the pizza sauce in the small microwave-safe bowl. Microwave on 100% power (high) for 1 minute or until warm.

4 Turn off oven. Remove pan from oven with hot pads. Cool slightly before serving. Serve vegetables with warm pizza sauce. Makes 6 servings.

Nacho Melters

What's better than eating a mountain of crunchy, cheesy nachos? Answer: Making and eating them with friends.

Ingredients

1 small tomato, if you like

4 cups baked tortilla chips (about 3 ounces)

½ of an 8-ounce package shredded Mexican cheese blend (1 cup)

2 to 4 tablespoons salsa

Cooked bacon pieces, if you like

Sour cream or dairy sour cream dip (any flavor), if you like

Utensils

sharp knife, if using tomato

cutting board, if using tomato

microwave-safe plate

measuring cups

measuring spoons

hot pads

How to Make It

1 If using a tomato, use the sharp knife to remove the stem. On the cutting board, use the sharp knife to cut the tomato into small pieces. Save until Step 5.

2 On the microwave-safe plate, arrange the tortilla chips in a pile.

3 Sprinkle the cheese on the chips. Spoon salsa over the chips.

4 Put the plate in the microwave oven. Microwave on high for 1 to 1½ minutes or just until cheese is melted, giving plate a half-turn halfway through cooking.

5 Use the hot pads to remove the plate from the microwave. If you like, sprinkle with the tomato pieces and/or cooked bacon pieces and top with sour cream or sour cream dip. Makes 4 servings.

Veggie Nachos

What's the best way to eat your vegetables? Pile them on a plateful of cheesy nachos as colorful toppers.

Ingredients

- 2   8-inch tomato, whole wheat, jalapeño, and/or plain flour tortillas*
- ½   cup canned refried beans
- 2   tablespoons chopped tomato
- ⅛   teaspoon ground cumin
- ⅓   cup shredded cheddar cheese
- ½   cup shredded lettuce

   Toppers: chopped tomato, chopped red or green sweet pepper, chopped red onion, chopped avocado, snipped fresh cilantro, sour cream

Utensils

cutting board

sharp knife

large baking sheet

hot pads

wire cooling rack

small saucepan

wooden spoon

2 microwave-safe serving dishes

How to Make It

1 Turn on the oven to 375°F. Place tortillas on cutting board. Cut each tortilla into 8 wedges with the sharp knife. Arrange the wedges in a single layer on baking sheet. Put baking sheet in oven. Bake for 8 to 10 minutes or until dry and crisp. Turn off the oven. Use hot pads to remove baking sheet from oven; place baking sheet on wire rack to cool.

2 While tortillas bake, put the refried beans, the 2 tablespoons chopped tomato, and the cumin in the saucepan. Put the saucepan on the burner. Turn the burner to medium heat. Cook about 3 minutes or until the bean mixture is warm, stirring now and then with the wooden spoon. Turn off burner. Use hot pads to remove saucepan from burner.

3 Spread cooled tortilla chips into the microwave-safe dishes. Spoon bean mixture on the chips.** Sprinkle with cheese. Put one dish in the microwave oven. Microwave on 100% power (high) about 1 minute or just until cheese melts. Use hot pads to remove dish from microwave oven. Repeat with remaining dish. Top with lettuce and your choice of toppers. Makes 2 servings.

*Tip: Substitute 2 ounces of purchased tortilla chips for the tortillas. Prepare as directed above, starting with Step 2.

**Tip: For more protein, sprinkle 1 cup chopped cooked chicken on the beans before adding cheese. Continue as directed.

Crispy Cheese Chips

Travel to a foreign land on your next snacking adventure. Wonton wrappers, used in Chinese cooking, make awesome chips.

Ingredients

Nonstick cooking spray
30 wonton wrappers
2 tablespoons olive oil
1 clove garlic, minced
½ teaspoon dried basil, crushed
¼ cup finely shredded Parmesan or Romano cheese

Utensils

baking sheet
foil, if making ruffled chips
cutting board
sharp knife
small bowl
measuring spoons
pastry brush
measuring cups
hot pads
pancake turner
wire cooling rack

How to Make It

1 Turn on oven to 350°F. Lightly coat the baking sheet with cooking spray. If you like ruffled chips, cover baking sheet with foil. Shape foil to make ridges. Lightly coat foil with cooking spray. Save baking sheet until Step 2.

2 On the cutting board, use the sharp knife to cut wonton wrappers in half diagonally. You will have 60 triangles. Arrange one-third of the triangles in a single layer on the prepared baking sheet. If making ruffled chips, place wonton triangles on foil, draping over foil ridges.

3 In the small bowl stir together the olive oil, garlic, and basil. Use the pastry brush to lightly brush the wonton triangles with one-third of the oil mixture; sprinkle with one-third of the cheese.

4 Put baking sheet in the oven. Bake about 8 minutes or until golden. Use hot pads to remove baking sheet from oven. Use the pancake turner to transfer chips to wire rack; cool completely. Repeat twice with the remaining wonton triangles, oil mixture, and cheese. Turn off oven. Makes 60 chips.

Snack on a Stick

Go ahead—play with your food! Get creative and skewer any combination of ingredients that will be a hit with kids in your crowd.

Ingredients

6 ounces sliced salami

6 ounces mozzarella or provolone cheese, cubed

1½ cups cantaloupe and/or honeydew melon balls

1 cup pimiento-stuffed and/or large pitted ripe olives

¾ cup cherry tomatoes

Utensils

cutting board

sharp knife

melon baller

measuring cups

twelve 6-inch bamboo skewers

serving plate

plastic wrap, if you like

How to Make It

1 On the cutting board, use the sharp knife to slice salami and cut the cheese into pieces. Use the melon baller to scoop pieces of cantaloupe into balls or the sharp knife to cut it into chunks.

2 On six 6-inch bamboo skewers, alternately thread salami, cheese, and melon balls. On another six 6-inch skewers, thread salami, cheese, olives, and cherry tomatoes. Place on a serving plate. If you like, cover with plastic wrap and put the plate in the refrigerator for up to 2 hours before serving. Makes 12 snack sticks.

Chicken Feed

This crunchy golden snack mix may look like something you would feed the chickens but its sweet, nutty flavor definitely pleases people.

Ingredients

¼ cup apple jelly or your favorite flavor jelly

3 tablespoons sugar

2 tablespoons butter or margarine

½ teaspoon ground cinnamon

1 cup rolled oats

½ cup peanuts or slivered almonds

¼ cup shelled sunflower seeds

¼ cup coconut

1 cup candy-coated peanuts, if you like

Utensils

measuring cups

measuring spoons

medium saucepan

wooden spoon

hot pads

13×9×2-inch baking pan

foil

large resealable plastic bag or storage container

How to Make It

1 Turn on the oven to 325°F. Put jelly, sugar, butter or margarine, and cinnamon in the saucepan. Put pan on a burner. Turn burner to low heat. Cook until the butter is melted and sugar is dissolved, stirring all the time with the wooden spoon. Turn off the burner. Use hot pads to remove pan from burner.

2 Add the oats, peanuts or almonds, sunflower seeds, and coconut to the mixture in the saucepan. Stir with the wooden spoon until mixed.

3 Pour the mixture into the ungreased baking pan. Spread the mixture in an even layer with the wooden spoon. Put the baking pan in the oven. Twice during baking, open the door and use hot pads to carefully pull out the oven rack slightly; stir the mixture with the wooden spoon. Bake for 20 to 25 minutes or until lightly browned. Turn off oven. Use hot pads to remove the pan from the oven.

4 Tear off a piece of foil that measures 14×12 inches. Using hot pads, pour the mixture from the pan onto the foil. Cool completely.

5 To store, place the mixture in the plastic bag or container; seal or cover tightly. Store in a cool, dry place for up to 2 weeks. If you like, just before serving, stir in candy-coated peanuts. Makes 5 cups.

PB Crunchers

After making these sweet and crunchy treats, count the raisins hiding in the candy-coated chow mein noodles.

Ingredients

- 1 3-ounce can chow mein noodles
- 1 cup cornflakes
- ½ cup raisins
- 1 12-ounce package (2 cups) peanut butter-flavored pieces

Utensils

waxed paper

baking sheet

measuring cups

large bowl

wooden spoon

microwave-safe medium bowl

hot pads

2 small spoons

storage container with lid

How to Make It

1 Tear off a piece of waxed paper. Cover the baking sheet with waxed paper. Save until Step 5.

2 Put the chow mein noodles, cornflakes, and raisins in the large bowl. Stir with the wooden spoon until mixed. Save until Step 4.

3 Put the peanut butter-flavored pieces in the microwave-safe bowl. Microwave, uncovered, on 100% power (high) for 45 seconds. Use hot pads to remove the bowl from the microwave. Stir with the wooden spoon until smooth. If necessary, microwave for 15 to 45 seconds more, stirring after every 15 seconds. (Or put the peanut butter pieces in the saucepan. Put the pan on a burner. Turn the burner to low heat. Heat until the pieces are melted, stirring all the time with the wooden spoon. Turn off the burner. Use hot pads to remove the pan from the heat.)

4 Pour the melted peanut butter mixture over the noodle mixture. Quickly stir with the wooden spoon until all is well mixed.

5 Working quickly, use 2 small spoons to drop the mixture onto the waxed-paper-covered baking sheet. Let stand at room temperature until firm. Transfer the crunchers to the container. Cover tightly and store in the refrigerator for up to 5 days. Makes 15 crunchers.

Rocky Road Popcorn

Make this popcorn coated with chocolate and peanut butter with your friends, then munch on it while you watch a movie together.

Ingredients

Nonstick cooking spray

12 ounces chocolate-flavor candy coating, chopped

2 tablespoons peanut butter

7 cups plain popped popcorn

2 cups peanuts

1 cup crisp rice cereal

1 cup tiny marshmallows

Utensils

large baking sheet

foil

large saucepan

measuring spoons

2 wooden spoons

hot pads

very large mixing bowl

measuring cups

storage container with lid

How to Make It

1 Cover the baking sheet with foil. Lightly coat the foil with nonstick cooking spray. Save until Step 4.

2 Put candy coating and peanut butter in the saucepan. Place the pan on the burner. Turn the burner to low heat. Heat until melted and smooth, stirring frequently with a wooden spoon. Turn off the burner. Use hot pads to remove pan from the burner.

3 While the candy coating is melting, put popcorn, peanuts, cereal, and marshmallows in the bowl. Using a clean wooden spoon, stir to combine. Pour warm candy coating mixture over popcorn mixture. Use a wooden spoon to stir well so all of the popcorn mixture is coated.

4 Spread popcorn mixture onto the baking sheet. Let stand at room temperature about 30 minutes or until cool. Break apart into clusters. Store in the tightly covered container for up to 2 days. Makes 12 cups.

Popcorn·Candy Balls

Make a bunch of these snowball-shape treats. Mix and form the popcorn balls with your friends—eat some now and send some home with them.

Ingredients

- 20 cups popped popcorn
- 1½ cups light-color corn syrup
- 1½ cups sugar
- 1 7-ounce jar marshmallow crème
- 2 tablespoons butter
- 1 teaspoon vanilla
- 1½ cups candy-coated milk chocolate pieces or candy-coated peanut butter-flavor pieces

Utensils

- 17×12×2-inch baking or roasting pan
- measuring cups
- measuring spoons
- large saucepan
- wooden spoon
- hot pads
- ruler
- plastic wrap

How to Make It

1 Turn on the oven to 300°F. Grease the baking or roasting pan. Put popcorn in the pan. Put the baking pan in the oven to keep the popcorn warm while preparing marshmallow mixture.

2 Put corn syrup and sugar in the large saucepan. Stir with the wooden spoon to combine. Put saucepan on burner. Turn burner to medium-high heat. Heat until boiling, stirring all the time. Turn off burner. Use hot pads to carefully remove saucepan from burner. Stir in marshmallow crème, the 2 tablespoons butter, and vanilla. Stir until combined.

3 Use hot pads to remove popcorn from oven. Pour marshmallow mixture over hot popcorn. Use the wooden spoon to toss popcorn and coat it as evenly as possible with marshmallow mixture.

4 Cool until popcorn mixture can be handled easily. Use the wooden spoon to stir in candy pieces. With damp hands, quickly shape mixture into 3-inch balls. Wrap each popcorn ball in plastic wrap. Store at room temperature for up to 1 week. Makes 24 popcorn balls.

Popcorn Cake: Put popcorn mixture into a buttered 10-inch tube pan. Press mixture gently into pan with damp hands. Let stand about 30 minutes. Remove and slice like a cake.

Choco-Peanut Swirls

Chocolate and peanut butter partner up, and the result is a lip-smackin' snack, perfect for satisfying an after-school sweet tooth.

Ingredients

- ½ cup graham cracker crumbs
- ¼ cup finely chopped peanuts
- 2 tablespoons butter, melted
- ¼ cup cream cheese (tub-style)
- 2 tablespoons creamy peanut butter
- 2 tablespoons milk
- 2 cups milk
- 1 4-serving-size package instant chocolate pudding mix

Utensils

measuring cups

2 small bowls

wooden spoon

measuring spoons

spoon

large bowl

wire whisk

six 4- to 6-ounce glasses

table knife

plastic wrap

How to Make It

1 To make a crumb mixture, put graham cracker crumbs and chopped peanuts in a small bowl. Stir with the wooden spoon to mix. Stir in butter until combined; save until Step 4.

2 Put cream cheese and peanut butter in another small bowl. Stir with the spoon until smooth. Gradually stir in 2 tablespoons milk until smooth. Save until Step 4.

3 Put the 2 cups milk and pudding mix in the large bowl. Use the wire whisk to combine mix and milk. Continue whisking for 2 minutes or until mixture starts to thicken.

4 Sprinkle 1 tablespoon crumb mixture into each of the glasses. Top with a rounded tablespoon of pudding. Spoon a small dab of peanut butter mixture on top of pudding. Swirl with a table knife. Top with remaining pudding and peanut butter mixture; swirl layers together. Sprinkle with remaining crumb mixture. Cover glasses with plastic wrap and put them in the refrigerator about 2 hours or until set. Makes 6 servings.

Apple Pie Bars

From sea to shining sea, apple pie is an American favorite. With all the flavor of a pie, these bars are really cool because you eat them with your fingers!

Ingredients

- 1 15-ounce package rolled refrigerated piecrusts (2 crusts)
- 1 21-ounce can apple pie filling
- ½ teaspoon ground cinnamon
-    milk
- ½ cup powdered sugar
- 1 tablespoon milk

Utensils

cutting board

sharp knife

8×8×2-inch baking pan

can opener

medium mixing bowl

wooden spoon

fork

pastry brush

measuring spoons

hot pads

wire cooling rack

measuring cups

small mixing bowl

wire whisk

How to Make It

1 Turn on the oven to 375°F. Take piecrusts out of the package and place on the cutting board. Allow piecrusts to stand at room temperature for 15 minutes. Unroll piecrusts. Use the knife to trim the rounded edges of the piecrusts to make 9-inch squares. Throw away the leftover piecrust.

2 Put 1 piecrust in the baking pan. Use your fingers to press the piecrust into the sides of the pan. Put the pie filling and cinnamon in the medium bowl. Use the wooden spoon to combine. Spoon apple mixture into the piecrust-lined pan. Top with remaining piecrust. Fold the edges under and press into the piecrust on the sides of the pan. Prick the top piecrust all over with the fork. Use the pastry brush to lightly brush a little milk over piecrust.

3 Place the pan in the oven. Bake about 45 minutes or until the crust is golden. Turn off the oven. Use the hot pads to remove the pan from the oven. Place the pan on the wire rack.

4 Put the powdered sugar and the 1 tablespoon milk in the small bowl. Use the whisk to combine to make a thin glaze. Use the pastry brush to brush glaze on the warm bars. Cool completely on the wire rack. Use the sharp knife to cut into bars.

Gooey Pizza Brownies

A festive topping of marshmallows, chocolate, candy, and caramel makes these fudgy brownies the perfect end-of-week snack.

Ingredients

Shortening

1   19.8- to 21.5-ounce package brownie mix

1½ cups tiny marshmallows

½   cup miniature semisweet chocolate pieces

½   cup miniature candy-coated semisweet chocolate pieces

½   cup toffee pieces

⅓   to ½ cup caramel ice cream topping

Utensils

13×9×2-inch baking pan

large bowl

mixing utensils

hot pads

wire cooling rack

sharp knife

How to Make It

1 Turn on oven to 350°F. Use the shortening to grease the bottom of the baking pan; set aside. Prepare brownie mix according to package directions. Spread batter into pan. Put pan in oven. Bake for 24 to 27 minutes or until edges are firm. Leave the oven on. Use hot pads to carefully remove pan from oven. Place pan on wire rack.

2 Top with marshmallows, chocolate pieces, candy-coated pieces, and toffee pieces. Drizzle with the caramel topping. Using hot pads, carefully return brownies to oven. Bake for 1 to 2 minutes more or until marshmallows are puffy. Turn off oven. Use hot pads to carefully remove pan from oven. Place pan on the wire rack to cool. Use the sharp knife to cut the into squares. Makes 24 brownies.

Cookie Swirl Cupcakes

If you like cookies and cream ice cream, you'll love these snow-white cupcakes swirled with chocolate cookie crumbs.

Ingredients

10 chocolate sandwich cookies with white filling

1 package 2-layer-size white cake mix

1 15- to 16-ounce can vanilla or other white frosting

24 miniature chocolate sandwich cookies with white filling

Utensils

2 muffin pans each with twelve 2½-inch cups

24 paper bake cups

large resealable plastic bag

rolling pin

large mixing bowl

rubber scraper

large spoon

hot pads

wire cooling racks

thin metal spatula

How to Make It

1 Turn on oven 350°F. Line the twenty-four 2½-inch muffin cups with the paper bake cups. Save until Step 2. Put the 10 sandwich cookies in the plastic bag. Seal the bag. Place the bag on the counter. Roll the rolling pin over the bag until the cookies are crushed into coarse crumbs. Save cookie crumbs until Step 2.

2 Mix the cake mix according to the directions on the package. Use the rubber scraper to gently stir the crushed cookies into the batter. Spoon batter into muffin cups, filling each about half full. Use the rubber scraper to scrape all the batter from the bowl. Bake according to package directions. Turn off oven. Use hot pads to remove muffin pans from oven. Place muffin pans on wire racks to cool for 5 minutes. Carefully remove cupcakes from pans and cool completely on racks.

3 Use the thin metal spatula to spread frosting on the cooled cupcakes. Top each cupcake with a miniature cookie. Makes 24 cupcakes.

Onion Hoops

You don't have to jump through hoops to make this snack. Just mix, dip, and bake before digging in to a plate full of these crisp onion rings.

Ingredients

Nonstick cooking spray

2 medium sweet yellow or white onions, cut into ¼-inch slices and separated into rings

¾ cup fine dry bread crumbs

3 tablespoons butter or margarine, melted

¼ teaspoon salt

2 egg whites

Utensils

large baking sheet

cutting board

sharp knife

measuring cups

measuring spoons

2 small bowls

wooden spoon

waxed paper

fork

hot pads

How to Make It

1 Turn on oven to 450°F. Lightly coat the baking sheet with cooking spray. On the cutting board, use the sharp knife to cut the onions into ¼-inch slices. Use your fingers to separate the slices into rings. In a small bowl stir together bread crumbs, melted butter, and salt with the wooden spoon. Tear off a piece of waxed paper and place on the counter. Spread about one-fourth of the crumb mixture on the waxed paper.

2 Place the egg whites in the second small bowl. Slightly beat the egg whites with the fork. Use the fork to dip the onion rings in the egg whites, coating completely.

3 Roll each onion ring in the bread crumb mixture. Replace waxed paper and add more of the crumb mixture as needed.* Place coated onion rings in a single layer on the baking sheet.

4 Put baking sheet in the oven. Bake for 12 to 15 minutes or until the onions are tender and the coating is crisp and golden. Turn off oven. Use hot pads to remove baking sheet from oven. Cool slightly before serving.

*Note: The crumb mixture will not stick if combined with egg white mixture. Use one-fourth of the crumb mixture at a time.

Zippy Potato Fries

Do you love crisp, crunchy fries? You'll crave these good-for-you potatoes, and so will the grown-ups.

Ingredients

Nonstick cooking spray

2   medium russet or
    Yukon gold potatoes

Salt and black pepper

Utensils

large baking sheet

vegetable brush

paper towels

vegetable peeler, if you like

cutting board

sharp knife

hot pads

pancake turner

How to Make It

1 Turn on the oven to 425°F. Lightly coat the baking sheet with nonstick cooking spray. Scrub the potatoes under running water with the vegetable brush. Pat the potatoes dry with paper towels. If you like, peel potatoes. On the cutting board, use the sharp knife to cut each potato lengthwise into 8 wedges.

2 Arrange potato wedges on the baking sheet. Coat potatoes lightly with cooking spray; sprinkle with salt and pepper.

3 Put the baking sheet in the oven. Bake for 15 minutes. Use hot pads to remove the baking sheet from oven. Turn the potato wedges with the pancake turner. Use hot pads to put baking sheet back into oven. Bake for 5 to 10 minutes more or until potatoes are tender and golden brown. Cool slightly before serving. Makes 3 or 4 servings.

Index